SUCCESSFUL MARKETING TODAY

Using Mobile, Social Media and Today's Internet

Steve Knipschild

About the Author

Steve Knipschild began his Internet marketing career in 1995 while living in Florida by learning how to create web sites as a hobby while working full time in a retail business. In just a few short years he had created his own Web Hosting Company, had become an Internet marketer, had owned and run several internet message forums and was running a Multi-Million Dollar E-Commerce website for his employer as the Online Service Director.

Through the last several years, Steve continued his Website hosting and internet businesses, but also owned/operated a rapidly expanding specialty retail brick and mortar store as well as having a successful online store for the business. In 2008 Steve Sold the Brick & Mortar store.

This allowed time for reflection, a change in direction, and a move back to the Midwest. After getting settled, Steve realized he was having difficulty finding businesses he needed to obtain products or services from locally, and that many business owners were not utilizing several of the most popular resources of "Today's Internet" including Social Media and Mobile Marketing which had helped make him successful.

One of Steve's strengths is that he loves helping people succeed! As a Social Media Marketing Specialist and expert on how to use Facebook, Twitter, Mobile Marketing and more of today's internet trends for business success, he now works with business owners make the most of their time and marketing efforts.

You can read more about Steve on his blog at http://www.SteveKnipschild.com.

Contents

Why Internet Marketing?

Over the last 12 years or so, the internet has become more and more ingrained in our daily lives. People use the internet to search for almost everything, including local businesses and other local information.

And with the explosive growth of smartphones like the iPhone, Android and Blackberries, this move to searching for everything online is just going to happen faster and in new ways.

If you're not reaching your current customers (and potential new customers) in the places they're searching for information, you're going to get left behind . . . by your competition that is.

In this book, we're going to look at some of the things that you need to be aware of when marketing on the web, as well as some of the ways that you can not only reach new customers, but get your existing customers to spend more money with you, and do it more often.

To view some 2011 statistics that will bring you up to speed on today's online marketing, please view the video on my blog at:

http://www.steveknipschild.com/2011-
social-media-stats-in-video/

The Move to Online Search

According to Google, 20 percent of all searches are related to location. And comScore reports that Google served up 10.7 billion searches in April, 2011. That means that approximately 2.14 billion searches were related to location – in other words, local search.

These numbers have been increasing every year over the last several years. Compare them to April, 2008 when Google served up 6.5 billion searches, which means roughly 1.3 billion local searches.

The bottom line is that more and more people are using the internet to search for local information, including businesses like yours.

And one of the advertising mediums that are being hit the hardest by this move online is Yellow Pages directories. Traditionally, the Yellow Pages have been the "go to" source for local businesses, and as a result if your business wasn't listed in the Yellow Pages, you would be missing out on a lot of potential customers.

But with the transition to internet-based local search, those searchers are becoming less and less likely to use the Yellow Pages. And not only because of the convenience and speed of the internet – they're also looking for reliable sources for reviews and other information about the companies they're considering which isn't possible with print advertising.

The Yellow Pages Dilemma

Yellow page providers realize that they need to do something to keep from becoming extinct in a few more years. One of the solutions they've attempted is internet-based Yellow Page directories.

These directories work much like the printed version. Your ad gets placed in whatever business category is applicable, on the assumption that people will use those directories to find local businesses. But the reality is that those sites have very little traffic – Google, Bing and Yahoo are the places that people turn to when they're looking for local businesses.

This is good for you for several reasons:

1. You have much more flexibility in how you present your business through the search engines than you do with online Yellow Page directories.

2. Your costs will be much less than what you would pay for an ad in the print version of the Yellow Pages, particularly compared to larger ads.

3. With local search marketing, you can update or make changes to your ads as often

as you want. Compare that to a print ad that can only be changed annually.

And on top of all those things, the internet gives you a much larger reach. Yellow Pages directories generally get distributed once a year, and only to households that have landline phones.

According to a study that the Department of Health and Human Services at the National Center for Health Statistics ran from January to June, 2010, approximately 24.9% of all adults live in households with only wireless phones. They have given up landlines completely.

That means nearly 25% of your target market may not even receive a Yellow Pages directory. They rely on the internet for virtually 100% of their searches.

And interestingly, even more children (29%) live in households with no landline phone. So as those children become adults and move out on their own, these numbers are expected to grow.

Connecting With Your Customers

There are a number of ways you can connect with your customers online, and if you want to get the best results you need to be take advantage of as many as possible. Because the internet makes it so easy for people to find the solutions they're looking for, you can't afford to hope they come to you – you need to meet them wherever they might be searching.

The most important place you need to establish a presence is in the search engines – specifically Google, Yahoo and Bing. Of the three, Google gets the largest percentage of searches (roughly 65% in April 2011, according to comScore) so it is the first place you should focus your efforts.

There are several aspects to having a presence in Google:

- The search results
- Google Places
- Sponsored ads
- Google Images
- Google News
- Google Video

These are all part of Google, but in many ways they are independent of each other. We're going to cover them all in detail in this book, but it's important to remember that each of them works separately from the others so you want to show up in as many as possible when your customers are searching for you. If you show up in most or all of them, it's going to create a strong impression with your customers, and make them much more likely to choose you over another business.

And keep in mind that the other search engines have many of these same features. We're going to talk about Google in most parts of this book because they are the largest, but virtually everything we cover translates over to Bing and Yahoo as well.

Google Places

Google has a service for local businesses called Google Places. This service lets you set up a profile for your business where you can showcase various things, such as:

- Special promotions
- Offers
- Photos and videos

Google Places also lets your customers post reviews about your business and you can respond to those reviews, creating a dialog with those people.

Your Google Places listing will show up when someone searches for the products or services you offer in your area, along with other companies offering the same things.

Now imagine how this process is going to work for a moment. When someone goes online to search for a company that provides the solutions you can, they're going to see several results in Google Places. What is going to make them choose one over another?

One aspect will be the ranking in Google Places. The top three results get the majority of their attention, with the first one getting more than the rest. So you want to be sure your listing is at or near the top of those results. (We'll look at some strategies for accomplishing this shortly.)

Another aspect is how much information is shared. If your company has a full profile with pictures, reviews, special offers and other information, it's a lot more likely to get the searcher's attention than another listing that just has the bare minimum information showing.

If this is a potential customer's first impression of your business, you need to be sure you're putting your best foot forward.

There are other important ways to connect with your customers beyond Google Places, however. Some we already mentioned – other Google properties – which we will cover in more detail shortly. But first, let's look at a relatively new way to reach your customers – social media.

Social Media Sites

One of the fastest growing segments of the internet over the last few years is what's known as Social Media. Facebook and Twitter are the two most well-known examples of social media sites.

Having a Facebook page is becoming more and more important, because people have come to expect it. There are over 800 million users on Facebook, and if you don't have a presence there you're missing out on a lot of potential business.

Plus, for many people Facebook has become synonymous with the internet. A lot of people spend most of their time online using Facebook, so if you aren't reaching them there, you may not have a chance to reach them at all.

Facebook started out as a way to connect on a personal level, but over the last couple of years they have added a lot of features that are targeted at businesses. You've probably already started to notice a lot of big companies adding "Find us on Facebook" to their websites, advertising and other places.

It can work just as well for local businesses, and in fact it can work even better. Because Facebook is by nature a place to be "social" a local business fits in much better than a big, faceless corporation.

Setting up a Facebook Page for your business gives you a way to connect with your customers "virtually" and it can help to create a real sense of community.

Twitter is another social media site where you should definitely have a presence. It's a little different beast, because the whole point is to post short updates (up to 140 characters at a time) so you can only share so much information.

It can be useful for sending out messages about special offers and other news, but more importantly it's another way for your customers and potential customers to contact you.

Your customers can send you messages, called "Tweets", via Twitter so it is similar to email in some ways. But because the messages are so short, it can be an effective way for them to ask quick questions or give you quick feedback, without having to invest a lot of time to do it.

Aside from reaching potential customers, there's another reason you should have a presence in these places – managing your brand. People will talk about their experiences with your company on the internet whether you're part of it or not. It's important that you are.

The newest entrant into the Social Media arena is Google Plus. Google+ (pronounced and sometimes written Google Plus, sometimes abbreviated as G+) is a social networking service operated by Google Inc. The service launched on June 28, 2011 in an invite-only "field testing" phase.

Google+ integrates social services such as Google Profiles and Google Buzz, and introduces new services Circles, Hangouts, Sparks, and Huddles. Google+ will be available as a desktop application and as a mobile application, but expected only on the Android and iOS operating systems. Sources such as The New York Times have declared it Google's biggest attempt to rival the social network Facebook, which had over 800 million users in 2011.

On July 14, 2011, Google announced that Google+ had reached 10 million users just two weeks after it was launched in a "limited" trial phase. After 3 weeks in operation, it had reached 20 million users.

After less than a day of being available, the Google+ iPhone app was the most popular free application in the Apple app store.

In November 2011 Google Plus introduced Pages. Directly from the Google blog:

> People + pages, better together – Google+ has been a place for real-life sharing, and Google+ Pages is no

exception. After all: behind every page (or storefront, or four-door sedan) is a passionate group of individuals, and we think you should able to connect with them too.

As of January 2012 Google CEO Larry Page trotted out an impressive statistic during last week's quarterly earnings call: Google+ now has 90 million users, double what it had three months ago. Even better, 60 percent of those users are engaged daily, and 80 percent weekly.

Managing Your Brand

One of the biggest hurdles for a lot of business owners to leap when it comes to the internet is realizing that people will be talking about your company whether you like it or not.

And that includes good AND bad. Mistakes are bound to happen in any business, but when they do it's quite possible that the story will wind up on the internet where anyone searching for your business can find it.

If you're not maintaining an effective presence on the web, you're going to have two problems if this happens.

1. The negative review could wind up ranking high in the search results, so whenever somebody searches for your business, this could be one of the first things they see. The review might be accurate if a mistake really was made, or it might be completely inaccurate, but that potential customer has no way of knowing for sure (and is probably going to accept it as fact).

2. You won't have a chance to explain the situation and fix it.

The solution here is to be a part of the conversation. In other words, engage your customers where these kinds of things might appear so you can try to correct any mistakes that were actually made, or explain your side if it's completely inaccurate.

We've already discussed two of the places that these kinds of discussions can happen – Facebook and Twitter. It's important that you have a presence on both, if only as a point of contact for your customers who are already in those places.

I recently created and posted a video that included 3 recent Social Media Blunders that occurred to some HUGE name brands that people use daily.

To see the free video visit:

http://www.steveknipschild.com/whysocialmedia/index.html

Imagine this scenario…

One of your employees has been dealing with a customer, and the customer is unhappy with the service they received. But instead of coming to you and giving you the opportunity to fix the problem, they go to these websites and post about the problem and how unhappy they were with your company.

If you don't have a presence on Twitter or Facebook, you might never know about it. But people who are looking for information about your company online could quite likely find that information whenever they search for you.

Now think about this...

If you are active on those sites, on the other hand, you can jump in and try to correct the situation. This is not only going to give you a chance to turn an unhappy customer into a happy one (who might also become one of your biggest supporters at that point) it's also going to add your side of things to the "record" of the situation on the internet.

Now when someone searching for you finds that review/complaint, they're also going to see your response, and the fact that you tried to correct the situation for that unhappy customer.

Which scenario would you prefer?

Review Sites

Another place that it's important to maintain an active presence is review sites, including:

- Yelp.com
- Where.com
- Citysearch.com
- Insiderpages.com
- Yahoo Local
- Google Maps

These sites are local business directories of a sort, which let people post ratings about reviews about them. Much like any other website we've discussed, you need to maintain a presence here if you want to be able to manage your brand and what people are saying about it.

One of the reasons these sites are so important is many of them have apps for the iPhone and other smartphones, so a lot of people use them to look up local businesses when they're on the go. If they find a listing with low ratings or bad reviews, they can just choose another one – the business owner will never know they lost a potential customer.

Just like Facebook and Twitter, you want to have an opportunity to either correct the problem or explain your side of it when these low ratings and review happen.

These sites aren't only about reviews, however. Many of them let you make special offers to your customers, in the way of discounts, giveaways and more. These special offers can be another great way to draw in both new and existing customers through their smartphones and other mobile devices.

If they are searching for a local business using one of these services, seeing an offer from your company will make them a lot more likely to visit. And if it's combined with good reviews and interaction on your part, it's going to cement their decision even more firmly.

Engaging Customers

Another aspect of managing your brand online is simply engaging your customers. This comes back to have a Facebook Page, setting up a Twitter account for your business and all the other things we've talked about.

This lets you connect with your customers without any of the cost associated with traditional advertising.

For example, if you have a Facebook Page where your customers can follow you, you can offer special promotions and other offers through it. A lot of people spend a great deal of their online time using Facebook, so you can reach a lot of people this way, with no advertising costs at all.

Let's look at a pub as an example. It's a Wednesday afternoon, and the week has been slower than normal. They've got an order arriving on Friday but still have too much inventory of a particularly brand of beer from the previous one. They've been building a following on Facebook by letting their customers know about their page. So they post a special offer on Facebook for that brand of beer, good for the next two days.

Do you think that might bring in a few customers who wouldn't have otherwise showed up over the next couple of days? Probably, and they more than likely won't stop with the special promotion, they'll order food as well. So a free promotion could turn a losing situation into additional profit for that business.

Facebook is one example of how to do this, but there is an even more powerful tool for getting these kind of short-notice promotions in front of your customers – mobile marketing.

Mobile Marketing

Mobile marketing is a huge growth opportunity for local businesses. More and more people are carrying smartphones that have always-on internet connections, and they're using them to find local businesses when they're on the go.

There are very few businesses that approach mobile marketing correctly, however.

Most companies have either no "mobile" version of their website, or if they do it's really just a smaller version of the same site. The latter is a little better option, but it's still not very effective.

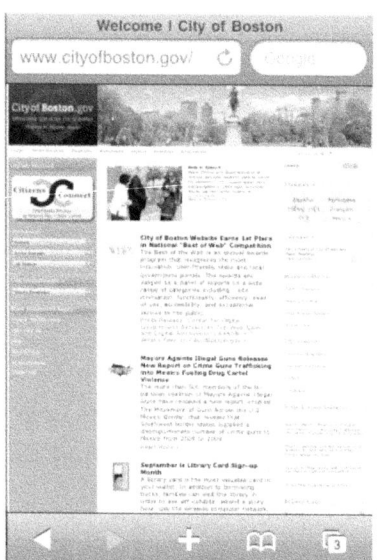

As far as the first problem – having no mobile-specific version of your website – this makes it extremely likely that someone searching for more information will simply leave the page and look for another site that's friendlier.

Look at the website for the City of Boston (on the previous page) as an example.

This is what a "regular" website looks like on a typical smartphone. It's practically impossible to read, and even if someone zooms in to see what's there, it's still not going to be very effective.

Having a mobile-friendly version of your website is a better option.

You can see what the City of Boston's mobile site looks like in the example below.

Much easier to read, right? This type of site might be fine for the City of Boston, since people are more than likely looking for information. But it isn't the best option for local businesses. After all, what are people looking for when they look up a business on their mobile phone?

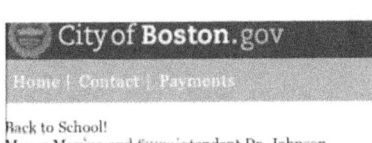

Back to School!
Mayor Menino and Superintendent Dr. Johnson welcome students back to school! For assistance with student assignment, transportation or other back-to-school issues, call the Family Hotline at 617.635.9046.
Back to School »

Most Requested Pages

- Parking
- Visitors
- Public Events
- Job Postings
- Elections and Records
- News and Press Releases
- Taxi Complaint and Lost Property
- Service Requests / Complaints
- Download the Citizens Connect iPhone App

99% of the time, they're looking for one of two things – a phone number or an address. They don't want to read the website or anything else; they're just trying to either call or get to the right location.

Let's look at an example of a much more effective mobile website. If someone searches for a local business on their smartphone, and winds up on a page like this, don't you think the chances are much better that they're going to actually call and/or visit as a result?

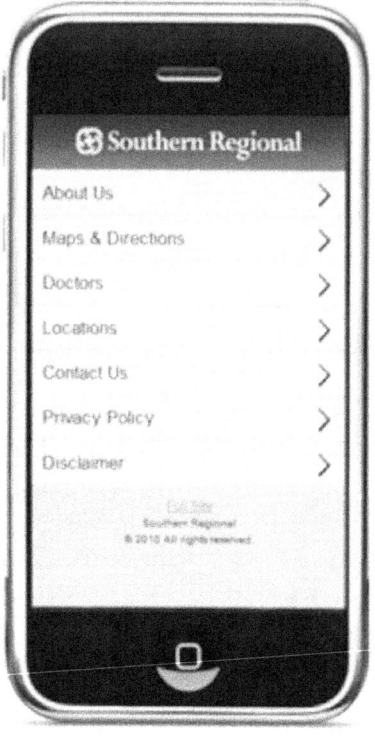

And that's not all you can do with mobile websites.

Most of today's smartphones have various other functions that can be integrated into a mobile site.

Many smartphones have GPS functions built right in. What if you could include GPS coordinates on your website so all your potential customer had to do was click on the link and it would open their GPS and give them exact directions to get from wherever they are to your location?

Or how about including all that contact information on your website so that customer could click another link and automatically have it all loaded into their phone's address book? Don't you think they'd be a lot more likely to make multiple visits to your business if the details were all loaded in their phone whenever they needed your products or services?

But there's one more incredibly powerful aspect of mobile marketing that is still extremely underused by local businesses – text messaging.

Text Messaging

Text messaging, or SMS, has experienced huge growth in the number of people who use it regularly. And it's not only younger people who are using it – it's becoming more and more common with older users as well.

Local businesses can use text messaging to engage their customers on a much more personal basis than even email marketing can provide.

There are two huge advantages to text messaging that really can't be matched by any other method of communication.

1. Most people have their phones with them virtually all the time, so those messages will reach them no matter where they are.

2. The vast majority of text messages get read almost instantly when they're received. Compare that to email that may go unopened for several days.

How can this work in your favor? Going back to our pub example, text messaging could work much the same as Facebook promotions, except it would be even more immediate.

If the pub was slow on a particular day, they could send a text message at 5:00pm and reasonably expect a response that same evening. There's just no other advertising medium that can reach your customers as immediately that is virtually guaranteed to be seen.

So does that mean you need to be feverishly tapping out text messages to all your customers every time you want to send something?

Not at all. There are services that will broadcast a text message to everyone who has requested to receive them from you. These services let you choose a number, called a Short Code, to use as your point of contact. Your customers just have to send a text to that number to sign up to receive text messages from you whenever you broadcast something out.

You can even set up an automatic response from these short codes, giving you the ability to offer an incentive to get people to opt into receiving those messages.

For example, a restaurant might offer a coupon for a free appetizer on their next visit by texting the word "appie" to their short code number. When the customer sends the text, they get a response virtually instantly with the details of how to get the free appetizer. This can be as simple as "Show this message to your server on your next visit to claim your free appetizer." But now whenever you broadcast a text message, they will receive it virtually instantly.

Coupon Sites

"Deal of the day" sites like Groupon and Living Social are another highly effective way to reach people through their mobile devices. You can advertise a special offer on these sites, which have apps for smartphones like the iPhone and Blackberry.

These apps offer what is known as "push" notifications of new specials. This works very similar to a text message – when a new offer is posted, the app displays a message on the phone.

Let's look at Groupon.com as an example, since it's the largest of these sites.

You list a special offer of some type with Groupon, offering a discounted price, a two-for-one special or any number of other special deals. Groupon posts the deal on their website, sends it out by email and pushes it to all the users of their mobile applications.

Because the offers are geographical, only people in your general area will see it by default. The users of the service benefit by getting a great deal on what you sell and your company benefits by getting a bunch of new customers who might never heard of you otherwise.

Plus, people outside of your immediate market can also view your offer, and buy it as a gift for someone who lives nearby. So you can reach people who don't even use the service via the people that do.

Keys to an Effective Website

Having a good mobile version is one aspect of an effective website, but there are several things that your main website should offer as well. Your website is responsible for several things:

- Educating your audience
- Branding your company
- Establishing your expertise in your industry
- Generating leads and sales
- Building relationships with your audience

There are also a couple of things it's NOT responsible for, however:

- Miraculously drawing in people searching for what you offer
- Replacing personal connection and interaction

One mistake that a lot of companies make is trying to cram as much information as possible into the home page of their site. This is a sure-fire way to overwhelm any new visitors, and in many cases they will just click away and keep looking.

Instead, use the home page to grab the visitor's attention and help them find the right page on the site for whatever information they're looking for. Think of it as a sort of "directory" for the rest of the site. You want people to be able to find what they want within 5 seconds of landing on your website if at all possible.

Try to look at your website from the perspective of someone who doesn't know your company and may not even know what you offer. If you look at it from the perspective of someone who already knows everything there is to know about your business, it makes it much harder to optimize for your visitors.

If you find it hard to distance yourself from your business this way, an effective way to do it is to create a customer "avatar" that you can use as a model for your typical customer.

Create a fictional customer who has most of the traits of your typical client. Give them a name, consider their age, their sex, what kind of knowledge they have about your product, their income, how many kids they have, etc. The more complete this avatar is…the better.

Then, whenever you are writing something for your customers, whether your website, an email, an article or any number of other types of content, write it as though you're addressing that fictional customer directly. This can really help to filter out the stuff that's either unnecessary or confusing and get right to the point you want to make.

We'll talk about how to get the people who are searching for what you offer to actually visit your website shortly (in fact, that's really the ultimate goal of everything in this book) but as far as personal connection and interaction goes, the internet has one very useful tool for this – email.

One of the most critical things you should be doing on your website is some kind of lead capture – getting your customers' names and email addresses so you can contact them via email.

Email Marketing

"66% of those surveyed said they had made a purchase because of a marketing message received through email."

- *ExactTarget, "2008 Channel Preference Survey"*

Every page on your website should have an opt-in form where people can sign up to receive your emails. While text messages, Facebook and various other methods of contacting customers are important, email is still one of the most widely used technologies on the internet.

Virtually everybody has an email address, and by building a list of your customers' names and email addresses, you can keep in touch with them on a regular basis to keep your company at the top of their mind.

You can send various things via email:
- Upcoming promotions
- Coupons
- Newsletter
- How-to information
- Anything else that would be relevant to your customers

Unlike flyers or other types of advertising, email doesn't have a per-message cost. Whether you send 20 emails a month or 2,000 emails a month, your cost isn't going to change by much, if at all.

What that means for you is that you can send an email as often as you like, and you can do it on short notice. So if you have a special event coming up or some other special promotion that you want to remind your customers about, it's just a matter of writing a quick email and sending it out to them a couple of days ahead of the event.

But it's not just a tool for sending special promotions like this. You can also use what's called an "autoresponder" to automate a certain amount of your email contact.

When a customer signs up to receive your emails, an autoresponder service will automatically send a certain number of messages at whatever interval you want. This lets you queue up a number of emails that will go out to your customers with absolutely no effort on your part.

You can use these emails to educate your customers about the products or services you offer, educate them about how to use those same products or services, or even just send monthly reminders that you are there to help if they need it.

You could even use it to send reminders of appointments or other due dates. For example, a dentist's office could send a reminder via email a day or two ahead of a scheduled appointment (not to mention a text message with the same information the day of the appointment) or a car dealer could send a reminder that it's time for the next oil change at the proper time following a customer's last visit.

And perhaps best of all, email is a two-way communication tool so you can even use it to ask your customers for feedback. There are various ways to take advantage of this:

- Ask them what their biggest questions are about the products you sell, so you can tailor your advertising and other promotions to answer those questions.

- Ask them what products or services they want or need that you don't currently offer.

- Get feedback and testimonials from them that you can use in future promotions

When you do this, you're not going to get responses from every customer who receives your email. In fact, you may only receive a couple of responses. But the responses you do get could help you make a lot more profit simply by providing the products or services that your customers are actually looking for.

How do you get people to sign up to receive your emails? There are various strategies that will work.

If you deal with people in person in your business, such as a retail shop or restaurant for example, you can have a computer or a portable device such as an iPad where people can enter their name and email address right at the point of sale.

This is considerably more effective than the low-tech method still used by a lot of businesses – a notebook and pen. Why have your customers write their names and email addresses in a notebook, when you can have them enter those directly into a lead-capture form on a computer? This puts them directly into your email service's database so you don't have to manually enter that information yourself.

Plus, if you use a device like an iPad you'll often get even more people who will sign up to receive your emails because they want to "play" with the device a bit. Even if it's just a matter of entering their information on your lead capture form, the novelty is still there.

Another effective way to get people to sign up to receive your emails is on your website itself. Add a lead capture form (known as an "opt-in box") to every page on your website so people can enter their name and email address no matter what page they might be looking at.

To increase the number of people who sign up to receive your emails, you can offer them some sort of incentive for doing so. This could be something like a free report or white paper that will help educate them about the products or services you offer, or it could be some sort of special offer or coupon that gets sent to them automatically after they sign up to receive your emails.

Or you could do both to improve your conversions even further. Offering a report or white paper has another advantage as well – you can use it to promote all the reasons why a potential customer would want to deal with your business as opposed to your competition.

That's not to say you need to badmouth your competitors. Just explain why your company is their best choice, and what unique benefits you can offer. If you provide them with a report that helps them learn more about what you have to offer them, and then include a bit of a sales pitch at the end, it can generate a lot of new customers for your company.

You can also use what is known as an "exit popup" on your website. This is a popup window that gets displayed when someone goes to leave your website. This popup can make essentially the same offer as the opt-in forms on every other page of your website, but it has been proven that these popup windows are more effective at convincing visitors to sign up for your email list.

The worst case is they will leave without signing up, but they were leaving your website anyway so why not make one last attempt at capturing their contact information?

Another way to get people to sign up to receive your emails is to use other advertising media to help promote it. If you send out flyers, include a brief call to action on each one letting people know they can sign up to receive special offers and other information by email by visiting your website. If you want to continue running Yellow Page ads even after reading this book, include that same call to action in your ad the next time you renew and have the opportunity to change it.

You could even add a message to the end of every customer receipt or invoice, asking them to sign up for your emails at your website.

Treat this email list as a valuable part of your business – because it is – and promote it anywhere and everywhere you can.

Multiple Methods of Contact

Your website should make it easy for your customers to contact you, no matter what method of communication they prefer. All the places they can get in touch with you should be easily found when they arrive at your website. This includes things such as:

- Your phone number

- Your address

- Links to other websites like Facebook and Twitter

- A "contact us" form where they can send you a message directly from the website

The more ways you give your customers to contact you, the more likely it is that they will. And different people prefer different methods, so make it easy for each of them to do it the way they want.

If you're really ambitious, and it fits the way you do business, you could even offer a live chat function on your website that lets your visitors chat with someone directly over the internet.

This is similar to a telephone conversation in many ways, except the communication is typed through the chat service instead.

This method of contact won't work for every business, but if you or a staff member is sitting in front of the computer for much of the day, it may work for you. And while it may seem a bit "antisocial" to some people, there are a lot of people who aren't comfortable calling and speaking to you "in person" but would be very comfortable chatting over the internet instead.

Promotional Strategies

One of the biggest advantages of using the internet to reach new customers is the low cost of advertising, and the speed at which you can implement, test and change things. There are many different promotional strategies you can use to both improve your rankings in the search engines and get your business listed in various other locations.

Press releases are an effective way to do this, for a couple of reasons. First, when you send out a press release, it is going to get listed on a lot of news websites quite quickly. Because you can include a link back to your site in the press release, it can drive a lot of potential customers directly to your site as well as help improve your site's rankings (which of course will also result in more potential customers).

And second, your press release might actually get noticed by a local newspaper and you could wind up getting some free press out of it. Many local newspapers are desperate for stories about people or businesses in their town. If you have something newsworthy in your press release, this is exactly the type of story they would like to print.

And the fact that you're local just makes it that much better, since they can contact you for further information if need be.

There are a number of press release services that will distribute your press release to various newspapers, websites and other media outlets. Some of the most effective include:

- PRWeb.com
- Webwire.com
- Marketwire.com
- PR.com
- WirePRNews.com

You submit your press release to these services, and they in turn broadcast them out to many different news outlets, both online and offline. The cost of these services varies, depending on the number of outlets they broadcast to and what other additional services they provide.

If you distribute press releases on a regular basis, you will not only be more likely to get noticed by one or more media outlets, you will also get SEO (Search Engine Optimization) benefits that can help your website rank higher in the search engines, and ultimately generate more traffic.

We'll look at SEO in more detail shortly.

Media distribution is another highly effective way to get more customers to your website. This means submitting articles, video, images and other types of content to various sites. When your content gets posted on those sites, it can make that content easier to find and improve your website's ranking – which ultimately results in new customers.

Video Distribution

Video is one of the most powerful types of media you can use. We already mentioned adding images and video to your Google Places page, but that's not the only place those types of content can be used. There are dozens of video sharing sites, the most widely used being YouTube, where you can also share your videos. Some of the other popular video sites include:

- Youtube.com
- Vimeo.com
- Dailymotion.com
- Veoh.com
- Justin.tv
- Buzznet.com
- Collegehumor.com
- Ustream.tv
- Revver.com

Some sites are focused on certain types of videos, such as Collegehumor.com which is focused on funny videos. Other sites have a wide range of topics, like YouTube.com, so you can post virtually any type of video.

Those videos could be a commercial format, or they could be something more educational if that style suits your business.

For example, if you operate a computer store you could set up a YouTube channel where you show people how to do various things with their computers. This would give you two opportunities to reach your customers.

First, people searching for a local computer store could find your videos on Google or another search engine, and they would see how knowledgeable you were. If you have a collection of videos showing various things they need to know to use a new computer, you'll have set yourself up as the local expert before they ever set foot in your store.

And second, you could use this as a benefit for your existing customers. They could get tutorials about their computer on YouTube, and you could even take questions from them via email, Facebook or various other sources and create videos explaining how to do whatever they're having trouble with.

Do you think that would help cement your customer relationships a little more effectively?

By submitting your video to multiple sites, you will extend your reach to more potential customers. Not only can they find the video on those sites directly, they can discover them through search engines like Google Video. You just never know where people will find your content, so the more places you can share it, the better.

Article Distribution

Article distribution is another highly effective way to reach your customers online. There are just as many article directories as there are video sharing sites, if not more. Some of the most effective sites to get your articles distributed include:

- Ezinearticles.com
- GoArticles.com
- Articlesbase.com
- WebProNews.com
- ArticleDashboard.com
- Article-buzz.com

Much like video sharing sites, some article distribution sites are more focused on certain topics, such as WebProNews.com which is mainly online marketing related information, while others cover virtually everything.

The way these sites work is you submit your article to get published on their website. You can include a short "bio" at the end of the article, telling the reader what your company offers along with a link back to your website.

The link in your bio has two benefits:

1. People who read the article will click on the link to visit your website, and once they do, they can then sign up for your email list, read more about your company or anything else that you offer on your site.

2. The link helps your website rank higher in Google and other search engines, so the more articles you distribute, the better you will rank when people are searching for local businesses.

The real power of these article sites is in the syndication features they offer. Most of these sites let other websites use your article on their site, as long as they leave your bio intact at the end of it.

So as other sites syndicate your article, you will get even more opportunities to reach your customers as well as more and more backlinks helping to push your website up in the search engine rankings.

And while all this is happening, you will help to establish your reputation as an expert. If someone goes searching for reviews or more information about your company, they will find all these different websites where your articles are posted. This will help make you the local expert on what you have to offer.

After all, if you saw the same author's articles in every magazine you read about a particular topic, you would probably think they know a little something about that subject, wouldn't you? Being mentioned all over the internet has the same effect.

Images

Images are another type of content that can help you extend your reach and get your company in front of potential customers. There are many different photo sharing sites where you can post these pictures:

- Flickr.com
- Photobucket.com
- Imageshack.com
- Imgur.com
- Picasa.com
- Smugmug.com

The value here is twofold. First, if it suits your business, you can share pictures of the products you sell, work you do or almost anything else. For example, an interior designer could share images of past jobs or before and after shots.

For someone searching for a local interior designer, a picture is worth a thousand words so having those pictures available for people to easily find can be invaluable. Google and most other search engines have mixed images into their search results, so you could end up attracting a potential customer's attention through those images.

But even if your business doesn't necessarily translate well into pictures, there are reasons you might want to distribute images to these sites.

One reason is for brand recognition. If people are searching online for what you offer and your company name or logo comes up in the search results, that will help to brand you in their mind. When they see your website listed in the search results, or find your Google Places listing on their smartphone the next time they go searching, they're going to recognize you over other companies that they haven't heard of.

And if you have pictures of your office or place of business online, it's going to make it easier for them to recognize when they get there.

All these things make dealing with your company a little easier for your customers, and when you add them all up it can make a big difference.

Paid Advertising

There are also a number of places that you can buy advertising on the internet, including:
- Pay per click (PPC) ads
- Banner ads
- Direct ad buys with other websites
- Facebook ads

Pay per click ads are one of the most cost effective. These are the "sponsored ads" that are displayed at the top and right of the search results on Google, Yahoo and Bing.

The way these ads work is you only pay whenever someone actually clicks on your ad, not when it gets displayed. And the cost per click can range anywhere from a few cents to several dollars, depending on what industry you are in and what keywords you're bidding on.

You create ad campaigns based on keywords that people who would be searching for your business might use to find it.

For example, if you were in the tool rental business you might bid on some of the following keywords:

- <city name> tool rentals
- <city name> power rake rental
- <city name> sump pump rental

...and so on.

You can set it up so your ads will only get displayed to anyone who is actually in your city or general area, which means that even if someone in another part of the country were searching for these phrases, your ads wouldn't be displayed.

Because you can control exactly where your ads get displayed, you can target the people who would be most likely to become potential customers very specifically.

And while the general keyword might have a high cost-per-click, when you are bidding on the local version of it (with the city name included) the cost is generally much lower. This will depend on the size of your city and the number of competitors who are also bidding on those keywords, however.

Banner Advertising

If you've been online for any length of time yourself, you've more than likely seen banner advertising in action. These are the graphic ads that you see on many sites. There are a number of ways to buy this advertising space. You can work with an ad network that handles the placement of your ads for you – choosing relevant websites, controlling what cities they get displayed in, etc. – or you can work directly with other websites to buy ad space on their pages.

You can even team up with other businesses in your local market to "trade" ad space on each other's websites. There are lots of ways to work with people who don't compete with you directly but would still be getting visitors who would be interested in what you have to offer.

For example, let's say you own a plumbing business. You could partner up with local electricians, realtors, contractors and various other businesses to share ad space on each other's website. Someone who is looking for an electrician will quite likely need a plumber at some point, and vice versa. Someone looking for a realtor may be looking for a whole bunch of other businesses because they're moving to the area and aren't familiar with it yet.

This can even be taken a step further by offering "finder's fees" for any referrals that you get as a result of another local business. You can set up a system that will track any new customers who click through from an ad on one of your partner businesses' website and wind up contacting you. You can then pay the person who referred them a finder's fee. If you set up these types of partnerships with several other complementary businesses, it can work out well for everyone involved without taking anything away from their own bottom line.

Banner advertising can be very effective, but for local business purposes you need to be sure that you are able to control where your ads get displayed. If you're an electrician in Portland, Oregon there's really no point is having your ad shown to someone who is surfing the web in Sarasota, Florida.

Facebook Ads

Facebook ads have some things in common with pay per click advertising – you only pay when someone actually clicks on one of your ads and you can target very specific people. The difference is instead of your ads being shown based on keywords that people are searching for; they're displayed based on demographics that you choose.

You have a great deal of control over the ads you display, so you can get very specific with who sees your ads. For example, if you own a gym or fitness club, you could create an ad that would target women between the ages of 35 and 50 who live in your city, have a college education and are interested in other health-related topics.

Then you could create a different ad that would target men with all those same demographics. And another one for each group between the ages of 50 and 60, or any other demographics you wanted. Facebook makes it very easy to put your ad in front of the people who are most likely to be interested in what you have to offer them.

And it also makes it easy to create multiple ads that ultimately bring potential customers to the same offer, but each ad can target a very particular group of people.

Whether or not you use Facebook yourself, keep something in mind – Facebook is growing at a much faster rate than other websites, including Google, so it is becoming more and more important that your business has a presence there, both in the way of a Facebook Page and advertising. This chart shows just how much faster Facebook is growing:

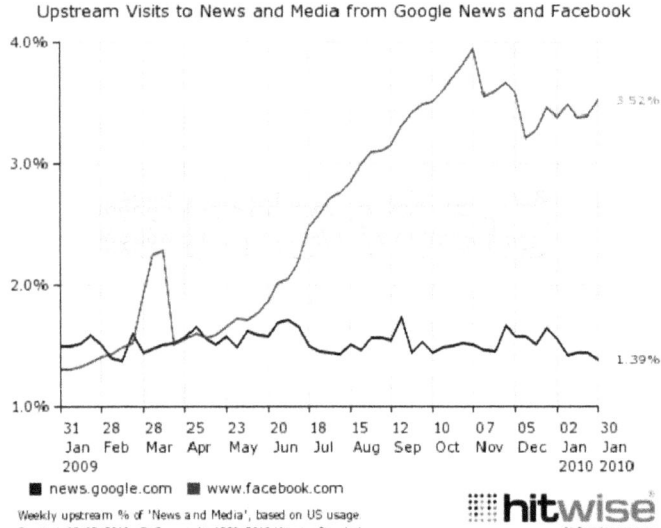

Upstream Visits to News and Media from Google News and Facebook

Search Engine Optimization

A lot of the things we've discussed in this book come under a subject known as search engine optimization, or SEO. This is the process of optimizing your site to improve your rankings in the search engines. Some of this involves things you can do on your site, such as using the "keywords" that your potential customers are using to find your site within the content of your pages.

There are tools that will help you determine exactly what those keywords are, such as the Google Keyword Tool. This tool is designed for Google Adwords advertisers, to help them figure out what keywords to bid on for their ads. But it works just as well for figuring out exactly what people are searching for. Because the things that people actually search for might not be what you would expect.

Let's look at a quick example. This screenshot shows a search for "Bellingham plumbers" (Bellingham is a city in Washington with a population of about 80,000 and 200,000 in the metro area).

This is just a few of the keywords that the tool returns, but you can see what people are searching for and roughly how many times each keyword gets searched every month.

Keyword	Competition	Global Monthly Searches	Local Monthly Searches
bellingham plumber		720	590
plumbers in seattle		1,600	1,600
bellingham plumbers		880	720
plumbers bellingham		880	720
plumber bellingham		720	590
plumber		1,000,000	450,000
plumbers		673,000	368,000
plumbing bellingham		590	480
plumbers in bellingham wa		73	73
plumbing contractors		33,100	27,100
bellingham plumbing		590	480
plumbing questions		4,400	2,900
plumbing repair		27,100	22,200
plumber seattle		2,400	2,400
plumber in bellingham		320	260
plumbing problems		12,100	8,100
plumbing services		49,500	22,200
bellingham map		3,600	2,900
pex plumbing		12,100	12,100
emergency plumbing		18,100	8,100

You can see the keyword phrase "Bellingham plumber" (the one we searched for here) gets 590 local monthly searches. That's 590 potential customers who are searching for that term every month, on average.

"Plumbers in Seattle" isn't directly related, since Seattle is about a two hour drive from Bellingham. But because it's relatively close, Google still shows it in the results.

You can see several other variations on the main keyword we searched for:

- Bellingham plumbers
- Plumber Bellingham
- Plumbers Bellingham
- Plumbers in Bellinghamwa

If you owned a plumbing business in Bellingham, you would want to work these variations into the content on your website to help improve your SEO and get ranked higher in the results when people are searching for those terms.

The other part of Search Engine Optimization involves things you post on other sites, like press releases, videos, images and various other types of content. The links that point back to your website from these places will help your site's ranking improve.

And the more sites that have links pointing back to your site, the better. Part of the calculation that Google and other search engines use to rank your website is the number of links, and the "power" of the websites they're on.

For example, if you had a link pointing to your website from a site like CNN.com it would be considerably more valuable to your ranking than a link from BobsWebsite.com.

There are various ways you can generate these links to your website. We discussed some of them, when we looked at media distribution. Articles, videos and various other types of media can include links to your website, so as you distribute them to more and more places you will generate more and more links back to your site.

You can also buy links on other websites. This is essentially a form of advertising, but instead of paying for another site to display your banner or paying for clicks on Google or Facebook, you're paying another site to link back to yours with the goal being better rankings.

Getting involved with some of sites we've already discussed elsewhere in this report can also help generate more links to your site. If you're active on Facebook and Twitter, you can use those sites to link to your website. Review sites like Yelp.com will also have links back to your website.

You can even set up multiple websites of your own, each with a very narrow focus. All of them can link back to your main site, helping to push its rankings up. For example, you might set up "mini-sites" for different product lines that you sell, or different services that you offer – each with a very specific focus. And these sites won't just be useful for linking back to your main website, they can also generate even more visitors and new customers as people find them in the search engines and various other places.

As you can see, many of these strategies work in tandem with one another. Media distribution doesn't just get your name out there, it helps with SEO. Being active on Facebook and Twitter doesn't just give your customers another way to contact you, it also helps your website rank better.

The more you market your business online, the more everything will compound to give you better and better results.

But keep in mind that SEO is not a one-time thing. You can ease back on the amount of content that you are distributing to various places once you've made an initial push to get your site ranked, but to maintain those rankings you'll need to do a certain amount of this on an ongoing basis. Otherwise, if your competitors are also improving their SEO, they could knock your site down and replace it in the rankings.

Tracking Your Results

Something that is fairly unique to the internet, compared to many other advertising methods, is how much information you can track about where your customers are coming from and which sources are the most (and least) profitable for you.

The nature of the internet lets you track the source of every visitor to your website, so you can tell how many potential customers are arriving from Google, Facebook, videos on YouTube and any other place you post your content.

You can even track these sources down to specific messages or media. For example, if you post a video on YouTube, you can code a special tracking link into it so you know exactly how many people end up visiting your website as a result of that specific video.

If you do any other advertising, like flyer or Yellow Pages, do you know how many visitors those sources are sending you? Probably not – there's really no way to track them with any accuracy, beyond asking every customer where they heard about you.

There are many tracking services available to you, ranging from free solutions to hundreds, or even thousands of dollars per month. One of the most effective is actually free to use – Google Analytics.

Google Analytics will track visitors coming to your website, where they're coming from and many other things. It will even tell you what keywords people searched for when they found your website in the search results.

This data can be invaluable to you because over time you can analyze it and work it back into your website to get even better results.

For example, using our Bellingham plumber example again, when you analyze your site's data you might find that you're getting traffic from Google for the phrase "Bellingham plumbing and heating" – a phrase you didn't do any optimization for.

Seeing that, you could hop over to Google and see just where your site ranks for that term. Let's say you find it towards the bottom of the page, maybe spot 7 or 8 (there are normally ten results shown on each page).

From this research, you now know two important things – people are already finding your site using that phrase and you could quite likely improve your ranking by doing a little bit of SEO for that phrase.

You might write a new article to add to your website that uses the phrase "Bellingham plumbing and heating" or you might just add it to a page or two that are already on the site.

Simply by doing this little bit of work, you would most likely start getting more visitors who are searching for that term because your site would move higher in the rankings.

Google Analytics doesn't just track your visitors, however – it can also track the actions those visitors take once they arrive at your website.

For example, if you have a lead capture form on your site to get people's name and email address so you can follow up with them in the future, you can track the people who actually sign up for your email list. With Google Analytics, you could track all the way from the click on one of your ads through to someone signing up to receive your emails.

And from there, you could use tracking codes to identify those people when they come into your place of business or contact you for more information. This lets you track the exact cost per customer by calculating your advertising cost versus the number of people who wind up doing business with you.

You'll know which advertising sources are most profitable, which ones are not working very well at all, and which ones are generating the most new leads. This is the type of detail that is extremely difficult, if not impossible to track through traditional advertising mediums like Yellow Page and newspaper ads.

The Bottom Line

The bottom line here is that Today's Internet gives you far better results than most traditional advertising methods. And it's not going anywhere, it's just going to become more and more important to local businesses as time goes on. If you aren't taking advantage of all the opportunities it offers, you have two choices – start taking advantage of them now or fall behind when your competition does.

And believe me; your competitors are hearing all these same things. Take a look at this slide,

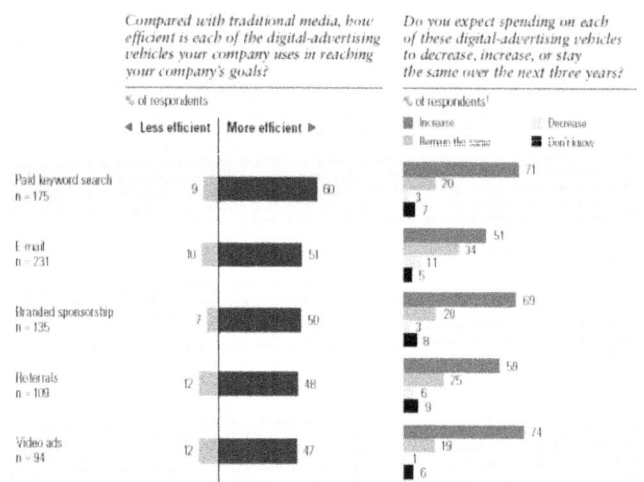

which shows the results of a McKinsey quarterly survey of business executive:

Notice that this survey was done in 2008. These results will be accelerating, not tapering off, as more time passes.

Where Should You Start?

We've covered quite a bit of ground so it's quite likely that you've got a bunch of ideas swimming around in your head, wondering where to start. But let's face it – is this the kind of stuff you want to do yourself?

You could probably figure all this technical stuff out for yourself, but is that really the best use of your time? I believe it's important for any business to work on their strengths.

I specialize in helping businesses get more customers by making them findable on the internet and mobile phones. If you'd like to learn how I can help you find new customers, as well as better engage the ones you already have, all at a much lower cost than most traditional methods of advertising, contact me today to set up a free consultation.

Steve Knipschild

http://www.SteveKnipschild.com
Email: stevek@steveknipschild.com

Social Media Links:
http://www.facebook.com/steveknipschildpage
http://twitter.com/steveknipschild
http://www.youtube.com/steveknipschild

Notes

Steve Knipschild | SUCCESSFUL MARKETING TODAY